Lookout Point Bible Stories

includes Reproducible Pages

Ages 8 to 10 • Grades 3 and 4

Course Description

High above the cluttered schedules and ringing cell phones of ordinary life is SonRock Kids Camp—an outdoor adventure camp like no other! As SonRock campers, your students will learn how their lives can be transformed by God's great love for them: *How great is the love the Father has lavished on us, that we should be called children of God!* (1 John 3:1).

Nothing challenges a person to examine his or her identity quite like an adventure in God's great outdoors. And with easy-to-make decorations, your church facility can be transformed into an adventure site: A pristine forest to explore. Fascinating animals to observe. Opportunities to learn new skills and reach new heights. But crisp mountain air and crystal clear streams of sweet water are only the beginning of what SonRock Kids Camp has to offer. Campers will build bonds of friendship with each other and with caring counselors as they discover that their true identities are not formed by where they go, what they can do or what others think. Like the apostle Peter, they'll explore who they are in Jesus Christ—the most important relationship of all. Because of His love for us, He is the rock upon which we can build our lives!

▶ As they watch Jesus call Peter away from his fishing nets, they'll discover what it means to be **Accepted by Jesus**.

▶ Later, when Jesus invites Peter to step out of the safety of a boat and onto a churning sea, they'll discover what it means to be **Protected by Jesus**.

▶ As they witness Peter's confession of Jesus as the Messiah, they'll learn how to be **Saved by Jesus**.

▶ From Peter's shocking denial and Jesus' redemptive forgiveness, they'll know that no sin is too large to be **Forgiven by Jesus**.

▶ Finally, as they discover how Peter's faith in Jesus made a lame man walk, they'll know the power of **Living for Jesus**.

This summer, send your kids to SonRock Kids Camp VBS—a mountaintop experience they'll never forget!

Gospel Light

Guidelines for Photocopying Reproducible Pages

Permission to make photocopies of or to reproduce by any other mechanical or electronic means in whole or in part any designated* page, illustration or activity in this book is granted only to the original purchaser and is intended for noncommercial use within a church or other Christian organization. None of the material in this book, not even those pages with permission to photocopy, may be reproduced for any commercial promotion, advertising or sale of a product or service or to share with any other persons, churches or organizations. Sharing of the material in this book with other churches or organizations not owned or controlled by the original purchaser is also prohibited. All rights reserved.

*Do not make any copies from this book unless you adhere strictly to the guidelines found on this page. Pages with the following notation can be legally reproduced:

© 2009 Gospel Light. Permission to photocopy granted to original purchaser only. *Lookout Point Bible Stories* • *Grades 3 and 4*

Gospel Light VBS
Fun in the Son!™

Senior Managing Editor, Sheryl Haystead
Editor, Karen McGraw
Editorial Team, Janis Halverson, Nicole Silver
Contributing Editors, Robin Blumenthal, Beth Gates, Josie Grim, Lisa Key, Susan Velo
Art Directors, Lori Hamilton, Jessica Morrison, Lenndy Pollard

Founder, Dr. Henrietta Mears
Publisher, William T. Greig
Senior Consulting Publisher, Dr. Elmer L. Towns
Senior Consulting Editor, Wesley Haystead, M.S.Ed.
Senior Editor, Theology and Biblical Content, Dr. Gary S. Greig

Course Overview
Bible Theme: 1 John 3:1

Daily Truth	Bible Story	Who Am I?	Bible Memory Verse
1 Accepted by Jesus	**Catch of the Day: Jesus Chooses Peter** Matthew 4:18-20; Luke 5:1-11; John 1:40-42	I am loved and accepted by Jesus.	"How great is the love the Father has lavished on us, that we should be called children of God!" 1 John 3:1
2 Protected by Jesus	**Wet and Wild Walk: Jesus Walks on Water** Matthew 14:13-36	I am helped and protected by Jesus.	"I am the LORD, your God, who takes hold of your right hand and says to you, Do not fear; I will help you." Isaiah 41:13
3 Saved by Jesus	**Tell It Like It Is: Peter's Confession of Christ** Matthew 16:13-17; Matthew 26—28	I am given salvation and eternal life by Jesus, God's Son.	"If you confess with your mouth, 'Jesus is Lord,' and believe in your heart that God raised him from the dead, you will be saved." Romans 10:9
4 Forgiven by Jesus	**A Rooster Crows: Peter Denies Jesus** Matthew 26:31-35, 69-75; Luke 22:54-62; John 21:1-17	Even when I sin, Jesus forgives me and gives me a fresh start.	"You are forgiving and good, O Lord, abounding in love to all who call to you." Psalm 86:5
5 Living for Jesus	**Lame Man Leaping: Peter Helps a Lame Man** Acts 3	I can live for Jesus and do the good things He has planned for me to do.	"For we are God's workmanship, created in Christ Jesus to do good works, which God prepared in advance for us to do." Ephesians 2:10

Contents

Teaching Helps

Sessions

Reproducible Pages

 **Focus on Evangelism**

Evangelism Opportunity
This symbol highlights portions of the lessons that provide special opportunities to explain the gospel message to children. Look for this symbol in the Tell the Story section of each lesson.

Make the theme come alive for your VBS students and they will be even more enthusiastic about joining in the activities! As leaders of the Bible Story Center, give yourself a new name inspired by nature: Wildflower, Twitter, Slider, Rock Steady, etc. Wear hiking boots and carry a walking stick! In addition to decorating your room, play the SonRock Kids Camp songs. You'll have as much fun as the kids—maybe more!

What's New This Year!

We've made a lot of changes this year, with all of you in mind! Responding to feedback from VBS directors and teachers all over the world, we've made some changes and additions to our curriculum. Here's what's new in the Bible Story Center for Grades 3 and 4.

Active Option and Table Option

We've got two very different ways for you to introduce SonRock campers to the main idea of each session: Accepted by Jesus, Protected by Jesus, Saved by Jesus, Forgiven by Jesus and Living for Jesus.

One is an Active Option—a quick and easy fun game—and the other is a Table Option—using a reproducible page found at the back of this book. Use whichever option best suits your group of campers.

You may also choose to use copies of the Table Option as a time-filler for students who finish other activities early. Or send the page home with your campers to keep the VBS fun going at home!

Creative Storytelling Option

You don't have to be a master storyteller to master these easy and fun options. Each day, a creative idea is suggested for breathing fresh life into the Bible story and to keep kids actively interested in the story.

SonRock Story Starter

Each day has its own quick and fun introductory activity to help children connect everyday life with the Bible lesson they are about to hear. No materials needed!

SonRock Kids Camp Journal

What makes summer camp more personal than a journal in which to record your thoughts and ideas? This year's student guide has a cool camp journal format that encourages kids to respond in a personal way to the activities they are experiencing at SonRock Kids Camp. The journal includes some just-for-fun pages that will help kids get to know their fellow campers, plus some bonus follow-up pages that kids can do to take home their summer camp learning.

Bible Story Posters on DVD

Not only can you post the Bible Story Posters in your classroom or hallways, but now you can show them on your television or monitor—perfect for those who tell Bible stories in a large group. Posters are available on the *A Rocky Road to Friendship* skits DVD.

Decorating Your Center

Lookout Point

Go tell it on the mountain! Tell your Bible stories from a campsite at the top of a mountain peak. A few simple decorations can transform an ordinary classroom into part of SonRock Kids Camp.

Level 1

Use these easy decorating supplies, available from Gospel Light. Display **Lookout Point Sign** at room entrance. Attach **Bible Story Posters**, **Memory Verse Posters**, large **Animal Posters** and **Wall Cutouts** to the walls. Add color with **balloons**, and **pennants**.

Level 2

For an even more camp-like atmosphere, set up a campsite in a corner of the room. Use **camping equipment** such as a pup tent, sleeping bags, camp chairs, lanterns, a cooler, etc. Set up a **Christmas tree** or other **artificial tree** next to your campsite. Add a few **stuffed animals** and **large rocks**.

Level 3

To create a sweeping mountain vista, use patterns and instructions available in *Camp Décor & More*. Enlarge the **Scenic Overlook Backdrop Pattern** onto butcher paper, paint and attach to the wall. Attach **fiberfill batting** to the clouds to create three-dimensional interest. Cut **poster board** into cloud shapes and glue additional fiberfill to both sides to create puffy clouds, and hang them from the ceiling. Use the **Wildlife Patterns** to make soaring hawks and perching owls on **foam core or poster board**. Hang birds from the ceiling or perch them in the trees. Add a few **Prop Rocks** and **Prop Trees** to your room and complete the scene with a **small campfire**.

Consider using a fog machine to enhance the stormy sea atmosphere in Session 2's Bible story. If your church has decorative wedding columns, use them for the temple in the Session 5 story. Use your imagination and whatever resources are available!

Bible Story Center Basics

You play a very important part in VBS, whether you are the leader in the Bible Story Center or a helper. Each day as you prepare the lesson, refer to the Bible Aims for Each Student. The aims help you know what learning will be taking place during your lesson. Study the Bible story Conclusion. This conversation provides an opportunity for evangelism.

The Bible Story Center is divided into three parts to help children learn important Bible truths.

1. Set the Story (5-10 minutes)

Choose either the Active Option or the Table Option as an introduction to the Bible story concept. Or use them after the story for fun ways to review the Bible concepts learned. If you only have 25 minutes for this center, you can omit Set the Story.

Active Option

This brief group activity is designed for groups of 8 to 16 students, with one leader for every 8 students. If you have more than 16 students, you can easily adapt the activity by duplicating it for an additional group of students—and adding another leader, of course!

Table Option

This fun activity uses one of the reproducible pages at the back of the book. You may also choose to use this page as a filler for kids who finish other activities quickly or send it home with students at the end of the session.

2. Tell the Story (10 minutes)

Each Bible story is about Jesus' friend and disciple Peter. Through Peter's experiences, including his mistakes, kids will learn not only about Peter, but about themselves as well. Display Bible story posters from *SonRock Kids Camp Poster Pack* for students to see while listening to the story. (These posters are also available on the *A Rocky Road to Friendship* skits DVD.) Telling the story in small groups is ideal, both for building relationships and allowing opportunity for interaction. But the story can also be told effectively to a large group—just make sure the storyteller is well-prepared and animated and that additional staff members sit among children to guide children's behavior.

SonRock Story Starter

Give Bibles to students to use during the story. Begin each story with a brief prayer. Then introduce the Bible story with a quick and fun activity to help children connect everyday life with the Bible lesson they are about to hear. No materials needed!

Bible Story

Each Bible story is written in language appropriate for third- to fourth-grade students. (Note: If you are teaching a mixed age-level group, the version found in this guide is appropriate for both younger and older students.) During the story, volunteers read brief Scripture passages or answer a quick involvement question. This helps keep kids actively involved in the story. For additional help, see the Storytelling Tips.

> **Drama Option:**
> Instead of telling the Bible story, have a team of volunteers come to each Bible Story Center and perform the Bible Story Skits from *Amp'd Up Assemblies*. Or older students may enjoy performing the skits themselves.

Creative Storytelling Option

Keep interest levels high using these creative options. Even if you're new to storytelling, these ideas will help you become a seasoned pro. Quick and easy, these options will help you make the story come to life for the staff and students.

Conclusion

After the main story, summarize the Bible truths for the students and relate the lesson to what students are learning about Jesus and their identities in Him.

3. Apply the Story (10-15 minutes)

Lead your students in applying the lesson to their lives through discussion and activities in the *SonRock Kids Camp Journal*. Whether or not you choose to tell the Bible story in a small or large group, these life-application activities are best suited to small groups which facilitate discussion. This time includes:

▶ Bible story review
▶ Memory verse discussion

Bible Story Center Basics (continued)

▶ Application activity and discussion
▶ Silent and/or group prayer

SonRock Kids Camp Journal

Get a copy of the student guide and look through it to familiarize yourself with its contents. The journal pages for each session begin with an activity designed to encourage students to think about the Bible story as it applies to their lives. This first page also has Bible story review questions to be used with an easy interactive activity described in the "Apply the Story" section of this guide.

The journal pages for each session continue with a fun life-application activity and the session memory verse. To reinforce the memory verse or reward students for verse memorization, SonRock Assortment or SonRock Animals stickers (available from Gospel Light) can be placed on the Sticker Page, found on pages 30-31 of the *Camp Journal*.

The journal pages for each session conclude with space for your students to respond to what they have learned in prayer. Allow up to five minutes of quiet time for students to write while you play music from *SonRock Tunes CD*.

If time is available, you may wish to have students make their own journals as special keepsakes of Son-Rock Kids Camp. The *Camp Creations Crafts for Kids* suggests several ideas for making journal covers. Or, ask your director if making a journal cover is planned in another activity center, such as the Craft Center.

In addition, if you wish to have students continue to use their journals at home after VBS is over, a blank journal page can be found in *Camp Decor & More* and also on the *Camp Director's Guide CD-ROM*. Photocopy several pages for each student to add to the back of his or her journal.

Effective Teaching Tips
Preparation Is the Key

▶ Pray for God to prepare the hearts of your students.

▶ Be prepared before each day begins. Have all materials ready for use so you can focus on the children and the learning that is taking place.
▶ Read through the entire lesson several times so that you know the lesson well.
▶ Know the Daily Truth and Who Am I? statements for each day and use them to connect each activity to the lesson's Bible story and memory verse.
▶ Learn and practice good storytelling techniques. (See the Storytelling Tips in this guide.)

Conversation Is an Art

▶ In addition to telling the Bible story, be prepared to make good use of informal conversation before and after the story. Suggestions are provided for each session to help you focus these moments toward the Bible aims.
▶ Be sensitive to each child's home situation and plan your conversation to include the variety of family situations represented in your class and among their friends.
▶ Review the conversation suggestions provided. Think of ways you might tailor or build on these ideas to meet the needs of the students in your class. Write down any other ideas or questions you might ask, and keep them with you during the session. Listening to children's responses will help you discover what a child knows (or doesn't know) about a particular topic.
▶ Plan to listen as much as you talk. Look directly at the child who is talking. Demonstrate your interest by responding to the specific ideas the child expressed.
▶ Know each child's name and use it in positive, loving, affirming ways throughout the lesson. Look for opportunities to express praise and encouragement.
▶ Stay with your students as they complete activities. Whenever possible, sit at students' eye level. They need to know that you are there, ready to help and ready to listen.
▶ Most importantly, pray for God to guide all your discussion with the students placed in your care.

Supply List

General Supplies

- Bibles
- *SonRock Kids Camp Journals*
- *SonRock Tunes CD* and player
- Bible Story Posters from *SonRock Kids Camp Poster Pack*
- Memory Verse Posters from *SonRock Kids Camp Poster Pack*
- SonRock stickers
- colored markers
- construction paper
- masking tape
- Post-it Notes
- scissors or paper cutter
- beanbag
- glue

Session 1

Rope Jump
- 10- to 12-foot (3.0- to 3.6-m) length of rope

Cabin Fever
- Cabin Fever Maze (p. 41)

Session 2

Save Me!
- large sheet of paper

Complete the Comic
- Complete the Comic (p. 42)

Session 3

Lifesaver Toss
- inflatable tube or other flotation device

Optional—
- whistle and other props to dress like a lifeguard

Swimming Rules
- Swimming Rules (p. 43)

Tell the Story
- Response Cards (p. 44)

Session 4

Time for Forgiveness
- Time for Forgiveness (p. 45)

Session 5

Paper Toss
- sleeping bag
- scrap paper

Straight Arrows
- Straight Arrows (p. 46)

Tell the Story
- Bible Story Pictures (p. 47)

Leading a Child to Christ

One of the greatest privileges of serving in VBS is helping children become members of God's family. Pray for the children you teach and ask God to prepare them to understand and receive the good news about Jesus. Ask God to give you the sensitivity and wisdom you need to communicate effectively and to be aware of opportunities that occur naturally.

Because children are easily influenced to follow the group, be cautious about asking for group decisions. Offer opportunities to talk and pray individually with any child who expresses interest in becoming a member of God's family—but without pressure. A good way to guard against coercing a child to respond is to simply ask, "Would you like to hear more about this now or at another time?"

When talking about salvation with children, use words and phrases they can understand; never assume they understand a concept just because they can repeat certain words. Avoid using symbolic terms ("born again," "ask Jesus to come into your heart," "open your heart," etc.) that will confuse these literal-minded thinkers. (You may also use the evangelism booklet *God Loves You!* which is available from Gospel Light.)

1. God wants you to become His child. Why do you think He wants you in His family? (See 1 John 3:1.)

2. You and I and every person in the world have done wrong things. The Bible word for doing wrong is "sin." What do you think should happen to us when we sin? (See Romans 6:23.)

3. God loves you so much that He sent His Son to die on the cross to take the punishment for your sin. Because Jesus never sinned, He is the only One who can take the punishment for your sin. On the third day after Jesus died, God brought Him back to life. (See 1 Corinthians 15:3-4; 1 John 4:14.)

4. Are you sorry for your sin? Tell God that you are. Do you believe Jesus died for your sin and then rose again? Tell Him that, too. If you tell God you are sorry for your sin and believe that Jesus died to take your sin away, God forgives you. (See 1 John 1:9.)

5. The Bible says that when you believe that Jesus is God's Son and that He is alive today, you receive God's gift of eternal life. This gift makes you a child of God. This means God is with you now and forever. (See John 1:12; 3:16.)

There is great value in encouraging a child to think and pray about what you have said before responding. Encourage the child who makes a decision to become a Christian to tell his or her parents. Give your pastor and the child's Sunday School teacher(s) his or her name. A child's initial response to Jesus is just the beginning of a lifelong process of growing in the faith, so children who make decisions need to be followed up to help them grow. The discipling booklet *Growing as God's Child* (available from Gospel Light) is an effective tool to use.

Catch of the Day
Jesus Chooses Peter

Scripture
Matthew 4:18-20; Luke 5:1-11; John 1:40-42

Bible Memory Verse
How great is the love the Father has lavished on us, that we should be called children of God! 1 John 3:1

Who Am I?
I am loved and accepted by Jesus.

Bible Aims for Each Student
During this session, I may

1. TELL that Peter discovered that Jesus loved and accepted him when Jesus chose him to be His disciple;
2. DISCUSS times kids might not feel loved or accepted;
3. THANK Jesus for loving and accepting me, even when others don't;
4. CHOOSE to receive God's forgiveness and to become a member of God's family, as the Holy Spirit leads.

Teacher's Devotional
Peter was an ordinary man with an ordinary career until Jesus came into his life. Jesus called Peter to follow Him and Peter responded. Did Peter know what he would be giving up or what he would be gaining by following Jesus?

As we look into Peter's life and experiences with Jesus, we will discover that ordinary Peter saw and did extraordinary things because of his willingness to follow Jesus. Peter experienced unconditional love and acceptance from Jesus. You made a decision to follow Jesus and lead campers at SonRock Kids Camp this week. You may feel ordinary and unsure of yourself, like Peter. Rest assured you are loved and accepted by Jesus! He has called you to serve Him and do extraordinary things by loving and leading the campers in your care. He will equip you to do all that is required of you.

As you prepare to meet your campers this week, ask the Lord to help you greet them warmly and be an extension of the unconditional love and acceptance Jesus has shown you.

1 Accepted by Jesus

1. Set the Story (5-10 minutes)

If you only have 25 minutes for this center, omit Set the Story.

Choose Either Active Option or Table Option

For either Option, use the conversation ideas in "Talk About" to tie the student activity to the Daily Truth that we are Accepted by Jesus.

Active Option: Rope Jump

Preparation: Lay rope down the center of an open area in your room. On a sheet of construction paper, print "Yes." On another sheet, print "No." Place "Yes" paper on one side of the rope and "No" paper on the other.

Procedure: Students stand on rope. Say a sentence that could describe a person ("I have a dog." "My favorite food is pizza." "I love to play basketball."). Students jump to either the "Yes" or "No" side of the rope, depending on whether or not the sentence describes them.

Materials

- 10- to 12-foot (3.0- to 3.6-m) length of rope
- two sheets of construction paper
- markers

Large Group Option:

Omit use of rope and "Yes" or "No" papers. Have all students sit down to begin the activity. If the statement applies to them, students stand up. Variety can be added to additional rounds by having students stand and clap hands over their heads, stand and jump up and down, etc.

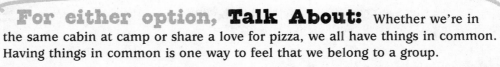

For either option, Talk About: Whether we're in the same cabin at camp or share a love for pizza, we all have things in common. Having things in common is one way to feel that we belong to a group.

▶ What are some of the groups, teams or clubs you've been a part of?

▶ Using examples mentioned by students: How did it feel to be (on the soccer team), Alejandro? (In the advanced music class), Brianna?

It feels good to belong to a group or a team. We're all a part of SonRock Kids Camp, and each of you belongs here! Belonging to a group is one way to feel accepted. But if you are like me, sometimes you might not feel accepted by others. Today we're going to talk about what we can do when we don't feel accepted.

Table Option: Cabin Fever

Preparation: Photocopy "Cabin Fever Maze, " making a copy for each student.

Procedure: Students complete maze and discover the phrase, "Being a part of the group means I've been accepted."

Materials

- Cabin Fever Maze (p. 41)
- markers

2. Tell the Story (10 minutes)

Preparation: Display Session 1 Bible Story Posters. Use Post-it Notes to mark Luke 5 and John 1 in students' Bibles. If Bibles are not available for all students, mark your Bible and ask volunteers to read verses as indicated in the story.

Materials

⚠ Bibles

⚠ Session 1 Bible Story Posters 1 and 2 from *Poster Pack*

⚠ Post-it Notes

Catch of the Day: Jesus Chooses Peter

Matthew 4:18-20; Luke 5:1-11; John 1:40-42

 **SonRock Story Starter** **It can be a lot of fun to pretend to be someone else. We can put on makeup or wear a costume, or just walk and talk differently when we pretend to be someone else. I'm going to pretend to be someone. See if you can guess who it is!** Imitate someone famous, someone from your church or a type of person that will be easy for students to identify (singer, basketball player, etc.). After the person's identity has been guessed, say, **Now think about someone you'd like to pretend to be.** Allow time for students to think. **On the count of three, everyone act like the person you thought of. Ready? One, two, three!** Students respond. Ask a few students to tell who they were pretending to be. **Today we're going to hear about a man who not only got to do something totally new in his life, but who also got a NEW name!**

The Fisherman

A long time ago, a man named Simon lived in a town near the Sea of Galilee. And it was on the waves of the sea that Simon earned money. **What do you think Simon did on the sea to earn money?** Simon was a fisherman! His brother Andrew was also a fisherman. Together, they worked hard six days a week—and nights, too! Fishermen often worked at night because it was easier to catch fish. During the day, Simon would work on his boat or his fishing nets. You see, back then, fishermen didn't use fishing poles and worms to catch fish. They used nets—big, strong nets made of coarse rope. Simon, Andrew and the other fishermen had to be very strong to lift the heavy nets full of fish.

But just because he was strong and hard-working didn't make everyone like Simon. Most likely there were days when he smelled pretty bad from working with fish and sweating in the hot sun. And even though he worked hard both day and night, he didn't always find fish to catch. If there weren't any fish, then Simon didn't have any money. Some people might have made fun of him for that, too.

The Rock

One very ordinary day, Simon was doing very ordinary things—perhaps working hard to untangle a fishing net or fixing a small leak in his boat. Suddenly Andrew came running up, so excited he could barely speak! "What is it, Andrew?" Simon asked.

When he caught his breath, Andrew cried out, "We have found the Savior God promised!" Simon was shocked. His net fell to the ground with a heavy wet THUD! *The Savior! Here?!* Simon and Andrew were Jewish. God had promised the Jewish people a Savior who would rescue them from suffering and trouble. The Jewish people had waited and

Skit Option:

For a fun alternative or supplement to this or any Bible story, ask teachers, youth helpers or student volunteers to perform the Bible story skits found in **Amp'd Up Assemblies**.

Large Group Option:

If you are planning to tell the Bible story in a large group, ask a volunteer to dress up like a fun camp character who found an old, old book about this fascinating man named Peter. (See description of Forrest R. Cool in **Wilderness Trail Theme Adventures**.) Every day, the character can excitedly tell what he or she has learned about Peter. Then students gather in small groups according to their age level. Leaders guide students to complete the activities under "Apply the Story."

Creative Storytelling Option:

Bring in a fish net (available at party supply stores) for kids to examine. As you tell the story, throw the net as if casting it in water to catch fish. If time allows, let volunteers practice throwing the net. You may wish to prepare and distribute card stock fish shapes to students and challenge them to see how many fish they can toss into the net at the appropriate time in the story.

waited and prayed for the Savior for HUNDREDS of years! So when Andrew told Simon they had found the Savior, Simon was amazed; he was shocked—he was stupefied!

I have to meet this Savior right away! Simon must have thought. "Let's go!" he yelled and he ran back with Andrew to meet Jesus.

Read what Jesus said to Simon in John 1:42. Jesus gave Simon a new name—"Peter." The name "Peter" means "rock." From that time on, Simon was known as Peter. Peter must have wondered why Jesus gave him this new name. *Maybe Jesus is calling me "Rock" because I'm so strong,* Peter may have thought. Later, Jesus told Peter that He gave him this new name to show that the people who followed Jesus would have a strong foundation—like a rock—that they could depend on when troubles came.

Then one day, Peter and Andrew were near Peter's boat, washing their nets after a very long, exhausting night of fishing. Not only had Peter and Andrew worked hard all night long, but they hadn't caught even one puny little fish! *I doubt there are any stinking fish left in all the stinking sea!* Peter thought, feeling sad and frustrated.

Suddenly, Peter realized there were people nearby. A LOT of people. A LOT of people listening to Jesus tell them about God. As Peter watched, more and more people crowded around Jesus. There were so many people, it was hard for them to see and hear what Jesus had to say.

Jesus saw Peter's boat and got into it. Peter must have been so pleased that Jesus got into HIS boat. Now everyone would know that Jesus didn't think Peter was too fishy smelling to be around! Jesus asked Peter to row away from the shore a little bit. Then Jesus sat down in the boat and continued to talk to the people about God.

Read Luke 5:4 to find out what happened next. *Pull out to deep water? Put out the nets?* Peter must have looked at Andrew in surprise. Peter figured Jesus didn't know how hard fishing really was! He told Jesus, "We've worked hard all night and haven't caught a THING! But, because You say so, I'll do it." Peter probably figured it was a waste of time, but did it anyway to please Jesus.

So Peter set sail for deep water. When they got there, SPLASH! Peter and Andrew threw the nets overboard. After a while, it was time to pull the nets back in. "Heave, ho!" Peter yelled. But the nets didn't move.

"Huh? What's going on?!" Peter yelled. "Put your back into it, Andrew! Pull HARDER!" They pulled and pulled as hard as they could. But the nets wouldn't budge.

Peter and Andrew carefully peered over the side of the boat. The nets were FULL of fish! Big fish, little fish, all kinds of fish wiggling around in the nets. That's why they couldn't pull in the nets. The fish made them so heavy the fishermen couldn't lift the nets. The nets were so full they were beginning to break! Peter and Andrew called over some friends in a nearby boat, "Come! Help us pull these nets into the boats!" The two boats were so full of fish that they almost sank!

The Fisher of Men

Peter was amazed. He looked at Jesus and fell down on his knees. "I'm not worthy to be near you!" Peter said, "I am a sinful man!" Peter knew he did wrong things. Things God didn't want him to do. Peter realized Jesus was sent from God, and being close to someone from God made Peter aware of how often he did wrong things.

But Jesus didn't send Peter away from Him. Jesus loved Peter and accepted him just as he was! Jesus invited Peter and his brother Andrew to be His friends and to follow Him. Jesus said they would help Him tell people about God and bring people into God's family instead of bringing in fish from the ocean! Peter and Andrew were glad to leave their boats, their nets, and all the stinky fish, and go with Jesus right away.

Conclusion

Just like Jesus loved and accepted Peter, Jesus loves and accepts us, too! That's why 1 John 3:1 says: "How great is the love the Father has lavished on us, that we should be called children of God!" Jesus' love for us can never be changed. He is like a strong, sturdy rock that can't be moved. We can build our lives on the rock of Jesus' love and acceptance.

Even today Jesus invites everyone to be His friend and follow Him. We don't have to be rich or smart or perfect. All we have to do is believe in Him and, like Peter, admit that we have sinned, that we have done wrong things. God loves us and wants us to be members of God's family.

Focus on Evangelism When we become members of God's family, God calls us His children! (Invite students interested in knowing more about becoming members of God's family to talk with you or another teacher after class. See "Leading a Child to Christ," p. 10.)

1 Accepted by Jesus

3. Apply the Story (10-15 minutes)

Bible Story Review

Let's play a fun game to talk about our Bible story. Students form pairs and play Rock, Paper, Scissors. After three rounds, ask one of the questions below (also on page 7 of the *Camp Journal*). Students who won two out of three rounds tell their answers to the question you asked. Repeat several times, asking a different question each time.

▶ **What did Jesus ask Peter and Andrew to do?** (Leave their fishing boats. Follow Him.)

▶ **How do you think Peter felt when Jesus asked him to follow Him and be His disciple?** (Excited. Scared. Worried about what might happen.)

▶ **Why do you think Peter had the courage to follow Jesus?**

▶ **What do you think is the best thing about knowing that Jesus wants you to follow Him?**

There are times in our lives when we may not feel like we belong, that we're not a part of the group—that we just aren't accepted by others! Give students their *Camp Journals*. Have students find "Accepted by Jesus" on page 7. **Every day at SonRock Kids Camp we will learn something true about who we are and how Jesus loves us. Today we're learning that Jesus loves and accepts each one of us, even when others don't! Because He loves us, He understands how we feel and He'll help us know what to do in tough times when we don't feel accepted.**

At camp, it's fun to write or draw in a journal every day so that you can always remember all the cool things you got to do and say. Every day at SonRock Kids Camp, you can add to your own camp journal. As time allows, students respond to question on page 7 of their journals.

Materials

▲ *SonRock Tunes CD* and player
▲ *Camp Journals*
▲ markers

Active Option:
Lead the Bible Story Review Game written specifically for each Bible story and available in **Big Rock Bible Games**. Make sure to coordinate your game plans with the leader of the Bible Games Center.

Memory Verse/Application

Students turn to pages 8-9 in their *Camp Journals* and read verse aloud. **Giving lavishly means giving much more than is expected or needed. Our verse also says that we are children of God. We become God's children when we choose to become members of God's family. Not just kids, but even adults are children of God!**

As students complete "Seen at Camp Today" activity ask questions such as:

▶ **When are some times someone might not feel accepted?** (Going to a new school. Joining a sports team when you don't know any of the other members. When someone else is being mean.)

▶ **How would it help a kid your age to know that Jesus always loves and accepts them?**

▶ **What are some things you can do to remember that Jesus accepts you, even when others don't?** (Talk to Jesus. Read a Bible verse or listen to a music CD about God's love.)

From time to time, everyone feels rejected or left out. But Jesus never rejects us! Even when others don't accept us, we can always remember that we are loved and accepted by Jesus.

Sticker Option:
Throughout the week, give students an opportunity to recite verses they memorized. For each verse memorized, give students a SonRock Assortment or SonRock Animals sticker to place on the sticker page in their camp journals.

Prayer

Play "How Great Is the Love" from CD as students take a few minutes to respond to the prayer prompts on page 10 of their journals.

Let's pray and thank Jesus for His love. Invite volunteers to complete the following sentence: **Jesus' love is . . . .** Close in prayer, thanking Jesus for loving and accepting us even when others don't.

Journal Reflections

Here's what worked today:

Here's what needs work for tomorrow:

My Prayer Requests

My Campers:

I experienced Jesus' love and acceptance today when

I can show Jesus' love and acceptance to tomorrow by

Wet and Wild Walk
Jesus Walks on Water

Scripture
Matthew 14:13-36

Bible Memory Verse
*I am the LORD, your God, who takes hold of your right hand and says to you,
Do not fear; I will help you.* Isaiah 41:13

Who Am I?
I am helped and protected by Jesus.

Bible Aims for Each Student
During this session, I may

1. REPORT that Jesus displayed His power and protected Peter when Peter was in danger;

2. IDENTIFY situations in which I can rely on Jesus' power and protection;

3. ASK Jesus' help to trust in His protection in every situation;

4. CHOOSE to receive God's forgiveness and to become a member of God's family, as the Holy Spirit leads.

Teacher's Devotional
In today's story Peter took a great step of faith and actually walked on water! But then he lost sight of Jesus and began to sink. When he cried out to Jesus, Jesus was right there with His hand outstretched, protecting Peter from the surrounding danger.

Have you ever stepped out in faith and confidence only to find yourself frozen by fear? How did Jesus help you overcome your fear? Following Jesus does not guarantee peaceful waters. There will be raging storms and many trials in this world. Remember to be encouraged and have hope, for Jesus has overcome the fears of this world (see John 16:33).

The campers you encounter this week may be experiencing their own storms, some even raised by being at SonRock Kids Camp. Trying a new activity may cause anxiety in a child. Interacting with other children may be worrisome. You can help calm these kinds of storms by giving the child the choice to watch for a while and then join in when he or she feels ready.

Thank God for each of the campers in your care. Ask Him to show you ways to point them to Jesus' protection and help.

2 Protected by Jesus

2 Protected by Jesus

1. Set the Story (5-10 minutes)

If you only have 25 minutes for this center, omit Set the Story.

Choose Either **Active Option** or **Table Option**

For either Option, use the conversation ideas in "Talk About" to tie the student activity to the Daily Truth that we are Protected by Jesus.

Active Option: Save Me!

Procedure: Ask students to name things at camp from which they might need protection (bugs, cold weather, bears, darkness, sickness, sun exposure, rain, etc.). List students' ideas on large sheet of paper.

When you have listed eight to ten items, play a game like Charades. Ask a volunteer to stand in front of the group. Whisper to the volunteer one of the items on the list. Volunteer pantomimes item as other students guess.

When students guess correctly, ask, **What could you use for protection from (cold weather)?** Repeat with other items on the list as time allows or until all students have had an opportunity to pantomime.

Materials

△ large sheet of paper
△ marker

Activity Tip:

If a student announces "I don't want to do this," the best response is matter-of-fact. "That's OK. Try a couple rounds. We'll be doing something else soon." More often than not, a student will enjoy the activity once he or she is involved.

For either option, **Talk About:**

Wherever we go, there are things from which we need protection.

▶ **What are some of the things you need protection from every day?** (Crime. Hunger. Weather.)

▶ **What are some of the ways you get the protection you need?** (Parents provide a house to live in and food to eat. Ask friends or teachers for help. Call police officers for help.)

Lots of times we think of the ways we protect ourselves from danger. But there are other kinds of protection, too. Sometimes we need help and protection when we are feeling sad or angry. Sometimes we need protection from doing wrong things. Today we're going to talk about protection that can help us in EVERY way!

Table Option: Complete the Comic

Preparation: Photocopy "Complete the Comic," making a copy for each student.
Procedure: Students complete their comic strips.

Materials

△ Complete the Comic (p. 42)
△ markers

2. Tell the Story (10 minutes)

Preparation: Display Session 2 Bible Story Posters. Use Post-it Notes to mark Matthew 14 in students' Bibles.

Materials

△ Bibles

△ Session 2 Bible Story Posters 1 and 2 from *Poster Pack*

△ Post-it Notes

Wet and Wild Walk: Jesus Walks on Water

Matthew 14:13-36

SonRock Story Starter Invite two or three volunteers to come to the front. Give each one a different endurance test: ask one to stand on one foot, another to hold out each arm fully extended to the side and the third to hold a book over his or her head. When students falter, offer a helping hand. **Good job! Those tasks may have seemed easy at first, but they got harder over time and each of you needed a helping hand. Everyone needs help from time to time. Today we're going to hear about a time Peter needed a helping hand.**

A Day of Surprises

Peter and his brother Andrew were two of Jesus' 12 disciples. These men traveled with Jesus, watched Him help people and listened as He told people about God.

One day Jesus said He wanted to go off somewhere quiet to have some peace and be alone with the disciples. So Jesus, Peter and the other disciples got in a boat and sailed off to a quiet beach. But people still found Jesus! Peter watched in amazement as a HUGE crowd of people gathered to hear Jesus talk about God. Over 5,000 men, women and children ended up in that isolated place! And then Jesus fed ALL the people with five small loaves of bread and two little fish. Not only that, but Peter and the other disciples were able to collect 12 baskets full of leftovers!

Peter was amazed. And full! He rubbed his belly. "What a great meal that was," Peter said when Jesus had finished talking to the people. "But now, I'm ready for that boat ride home!" he continued.

A Night on the Lake

Read what Jesus did in Matthew 14:22. Jesus asked the disciples to go on without Him because He wanted to spend some quiet time alone to pray and talk with God.

But when the disciples got in the boat, a strong wind began to blow. The boat rocked and swayed. The sails snapped back and forth with the wind. One of the ropes whipped across the deck. "Whoa! Catch that rope!" someone yelled. The disciples were drenched from the water that surged over the sides of the boat. Slipping and sliding across the deck, the disciples held on to the ropes and rails to keep from falling out of the boat!

A Walk to Remember

Then, in the middle of the night, between three and six o'clock in the morning, one of the men saw something out on the wild waves. "Look there," he cried out. Everyone turned to look where he was pointing. Peter squinted into the wind, trying to see. Yes, there was something out there on the water. It wasn't another boat . . . It was a person! And the person was walking on top of the water!

Storytelling Tip:

Teach from the Bible, not your curriculum. Students need to see you as a teacher of God's Word—not merely a reader of a curriculum product. Have your Bible open in front of you throughout the story and clearly state that the story is true: "This story happened to real people. We know the story is true because it comes from God's Word, the Bible."

Creative Storytelling Option:

Divide children into groups and assign each group a different sound effect and/or motion: water sounds (saying "psh, psh, psh"), eating (making crunching noises), wind (saying "whoo, whoo" or whistling), etc. Lead students to make sounds and motions at appropriate times during story. As you describe the stormy waters, mist students with water from a spray bottle.

What do you think the disciples thought of that? Read Matthew 14:26. A GHOST?! Everyone gasped and their hearts beat faster. *No, it can't be!* Peter may have thought. *But what else could it be? People can't walk on water!* Peter squinted harder, trying to better see what it was.

Then he heard a voice, "Have courage! It is I! Don't be afraid."

"I know that voice," Peter may have shouted. "It's Jesus!" Peter was so excited. His friend, Jesus, was walking on the water. It was the coolest, most amazing thing Peter had ever seen. And since he'd been with Jesus, he'd seen some amazing things!

The other disciples looked at Peter in surprise. "Peter, are you crazy? It can't be Jesus. Nobody can walk on water! It must be a ghost," they said.

But Peter was sure. Peter leaned into the wind and shouted with all his might, "Lord, if You really are Jesus, tell me to come to You on the water!" The other disciples stared at him in fear. Andrew put a hand on Peter's shoulder to stop him.

Then the disciples heard one simple word. "Come," Jesus said. And over the side of the boat Peter went. Peter stared straight at Jesus. He walked right on top of the tossing waves, excited and overjoyed to see his friend, the amazing Jesus.

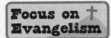

Then Peter felt the wind push against him. *The wind…* Peter remembered the wild wind that had rocked the boat all night. *The boat… The water… I'm walking on water!* Peter felt panic rise in his throat. *I'm walking on WATER?? I can't walk on WATER!* Peter looked away from Jesus. He looked down at the wild waves at his feet. And icy cold fear crawled through his body. Peter began to sink, sliding down into the waves he had just been walking on.

Peter gasped and struggled to keep his head above water. He reached out a hand, desperately grasping for Jesus. He sputtered and spit water from his mouth. "Lord, save me!" He cried.

Jesus reached down and grabbed Peter's cold, wet hand. Immediately, Peter rose out of the water and was next to Jesus. "Oh, you of little faith. Why did you doubt me?" Jesus asked. Peter hung his head in shame.

Cold and tired, exhausted from fear, Peter clung to Jesus as Jesus walked him back to the boat and they climbed in. Immediately, the wind died down and everything was quiet and still in the boat.

The other disciples stood still in shock for a moment. **What do you think the other disciples said next? Read Matthew 14:33 to find out.** Peter and the other disciples realized Jesus must be sent from God. Only someone with God's power could do what Jesus had just done.

After the boat landed, some people recognized Jesus and spread the word that Jesus had come. People from the surrounding villages came to see Jesus and asked Him to heal those who were sick. All the sick people who came to see Jesus were healed!

Conclusion

Peter realized that Jesus is powerful enough to walk on water and that Jesus loved him enough to protect him from the dangerous water. Bad things may happen to us, too. But in every situation, we have someone strong to help us. Jesus' power and love are like a solid rock—He is always ready to help us, just like He protected Peter. We can believe God's promise in Isaiah 41:13 to help us remember what to do when we are afraid.

Focus on Evangelism Jesus loves us so much, He made it possible for us to be members of God's family. (Invite students interested in knowing more about becoming members of God's family to talk with you or another teacher after class. See "Leading a Child to Christ," p. 10.)

3. Apply the Story (10-15 minutes)

Bible Story Review

Let's have some fun while we talk about our Bible story today. Students walk around the room as you play "SonRock Kids Camp" from CD. After a few moments, stop the music. Student standing closest to the CD player when you stop the music answers one of the questions below (also on page 11 of the *Camp Journals*) or chooses a volunteer to answer. Repeat with other places (chalkboard, door, bookshelf, window, etc.) as time permits, asking a different question each time.

▶ **Why do you think Peter had courage to step out of the boat and walk to Jesus?**

▶ **What words would you use to describe Peter at the beginning of the story? In the middle? At the end?**

▶ **What amazing truth about Jesus did Peter discover?**

Jesus was able to walk on the water because of His great power. Peter was able to walk on the water, too, when he trusted in Jesus' power. But even when Peter started to sink because of his doubt, all he needed to do was call out to Jesus. Jesus loved Peter enough to protect him from drowning in the dangerous water. Have students find "Protected by Jesus" on page 11. **Today the truth we are learning is that we need protection and help, and Jesus is the only One who can always help us. Jesus is more powerful than anything! We can trust in Jesus' love and power, and trust that He will protect us, even when bad things happen.** As time permits, students respond to question on page 11 of their journals.

Materials

▲ *SonRock Tunes CD* and player
▲ *Camp Journals*
▲ markers
▲ large sheet of paper

Memory Verse/Application

Students turn to pages 12-13 in their *Camp Journals* and read verse aloud. **What promise does God give us in this verse?** (That He will help us.) **What does this verse tell us to do?** (Not to be afraid.) **How would you say the main idea of this verse in your own words? I'm so glad that someone powerful enough to walk on water loves us enough to protect us!**

As students complete "'Water' Worries?" activity ask questions such as:

▶ **When are some times a kid your age might feel scared, worried or vulnerable?** (When someone else is being mean. When a loved one is sick. When having to do something difficult.)

▶ **What can you do to feel better when you're feeling scared, worried or vulnerable?** (Talk to someone you love. Pray. Go be with a friend.)

▶ **What are some of the ways Jesus uses other people to give us help and protection?**

Ask volunteers to share what they marked on their pages. **Jesus does not promise that we won't have tough times in our lives. But no matter what happens in our lives, Jesus will be with us. Even though there will be times when we feel scared or alone, we can remember that Jesus is powerful and that He can protect us.**

Acceptance vs. Approval:

While we may not always approve of a student's behavior, we can always accept that student as a worthwhile person. Approval and acceptance are two different concepts. Acceptance means recognizing another person's worth and feelings without judging or condemning. It's based on the fact that God loves and accepts each of us. Acceptance means caring enough to help the student find ways to overcome disruptive or destructive behavior.

Prayer

Play "Walking on the Water" from CD as students take a few minutes to respond to the prayer prompts on page 14 of their journals.

Ask students to name reasons we can know that Jesus is powerful. Write responses on large sheet of paper. **Because Jesus is so powerful, we know that He can be with us in EVERY situation!** Close in prayer, asking Jesus for help to trust in His protection in every situation.

Journal Reflections

Here's what worked today:

Here's what needs work for tomorrow:

My Prayer Requests

Notes for Tomorrow:

I experienced Jesus' help and protection today when

One child to whom I can model Jesus' help and protection is

Tell It Like It Is
Peter's Confession of Christ

Scripture
Matthew 16:13-17; Matthew 26—28

Bible Memory Verse
If you confess with your mouth, "Jesus is Lord," and believe in your heart that God raised him from the dead, you will be saved. Romans 10:9

Who Am I?
I am given salvation and eternal life by Jesus, God's Son.

Bible Aims for Each Student
During this session, I may

1. TELL about the time Peter confessed that Jesus is the Savior;

2. DISCUSS what "salvation" and "eternal life" mean in my life;

3. THANK Jesus for His gifts of salvation and eternal life;

4. CHOOSE to receive God's forgiveness and to become a member of God's family, as the Holy Spirit leads.

Teacher's Devotional
Today SonRock campers will explore what it means to be saved. As a Jewish man, Peter had been taught about God's promised Savior. The realization that Jesus was that very Savior came to Peter through spending time with Jesus and by revelation of the Holy Spirit.

Just like Peter, each one of us has to decide who we believe Jesus is. Believing Jesus is the Christ causes a radical change in our lives. Our sins are forgiven and we are assured eternal life. Even more, proclaiming Jesus as Savior and Lord also gives us the incredible opportunity to fulfill the purpose for which we were created: to know Christ and to make Him known.

The idea of needing to be "saved" may be foreign to your campers. Read carefully the child-level explanations provided in this lesson. Pray for opportunities to help them understand the need to accept God's amazing gifts of salvation and eternal life. Think about the perfection of Jesus and theimmeasurable love He displayed when He willingly paid the price for your sin and the sins of your campers. Ask Him to help you love each camper the way He does.

Saved by Jesus

1. Set the Story (5-10 minutes)

If you only have 25 minutes for this center, omit Set the Story.

Choose Either Active Option or Table Option
For either Option, use the conversation ideas in "Talk About" to tie the student activity to the Daily Truth that we are Saved by Jesus.

Active Option: Lifesaver Toss

Preparation: Inflate tube if needed. (Optional: Wear whistle around neck and use it while leading activity. Dress like a lifeguard.)

Procedure: Students stand in a group and raise their arms over their heads. Toss inflatable tube or other flotation device to try to "ring" an upraised arm. Student whose arm is "ringed" names a rule when swimming, or a general camp rule. Repeat until six to eight rules have been named.

Materials

⚠ inflatable tube or other flotation device

Optional—

⚠ whistle and other props to dress like a lifeguard

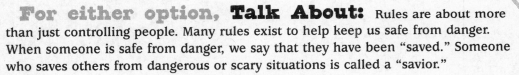

For either option, Talk About: Rules are about more than just controlling people. Many rules exist to help keep us safe from danger. When someone is safe from danger, we say that they have been "saved." Someone who saves others from dangerous or scary situations is called a "savior."

▶ **What is a rule that keeps you safe at home, at school, or anywhere?** (Look both ways before crossing the street. Use the handrail. Buckle your seatbelt. Don't talk to strangers.)

▶ **When is a time you've been saved from something dangerous or scary?**

▶ **When you don't follow the rules, there are consequences!** At camp, you might get KP (Kitchen Patrol) or have to sit out during swim time as punishment. There are consequences to breaking God's rules, too. We don't get to enjoy the good things God has planned for us because He loves us.

Because we all break God's rules, we need someone, a Savior, to save us from the consequences. Today we're going to talk about how people in Bible times came to know who this Savior is and how we can get to know Him, too.

Table Option: Swimming Rules

Preparation: Photocopy "Swimming Rules," making a copy for each student.

Procedure: Students unscramble the words in the sign and respond to the question at the bottom of the sheet. As time permits, students tell their responses.

Materials

⚠ Swimming Rules (p. 43)

⚠ markers

2. Tell the Story (10 minutes)

Preparation: Display Session 3 Bible Story Poster. Use Post-it Notes to mark Matthew 16 in students' Bibles. If Bibles are not available for all students, mark your Bible and ask volunteers to read verses as indicated in the story.

Materials

⚠ Bibles

⚠ Session 3 Bible Story Poster from *Poster Pack*

⚠ Post-it Notes

Tell It Like It Is: Peter's Confession of Christ Matthew 16:13-17; Matthew 26—28

Listen to the words I say, and if it's something you love a lot, spread your hands out like this. Demonstrate action. **If it's something you love just a little, hold your hands very close together like this.** Demonstrate action. **If it's something you love halfway between a lot and a little, spread your hands apart just a short distance. Are you ready?** Name some or all of the following items, pausing after each to let students make appropriate actions: ice cream, broccoli, skateboarding, pizza, homework, basketball. Modify the list of words to reflect the likes and dislikes of the students in your group. **I can tell there are some things that you REALLY love! Today we're going to hear about Someone who loves us so much, He made a way for us to join God's family and live forever!**

Many False Gods

One day Peter and the other disciples were walking with Jesus in an area called Caesarea Philippi. The people of Caesarea Philippi worshiped many idols—false gods. But Peter and the rest of the disciples were used to Jerusalem, where people worshiped the only real God. Peter may have even wondered, *Why would Jesus want to come here?*

A Prophet?

As they were walking along, however, Jesus turned to the disciples and asked them an important question. **Read Matthew 16:13 to read Jesus' question.**

"Who do the people say I am?" Jesus asked.

Wow! That probably wasn't a question Peter was expecting. But it was easy enough to answer. After all, everywhere he and the other disciples went, people were talking about Jesus!

(Optional: Ask students holding cards 1-4 to read answers aloud.) "Some people think you're John the Baptist," one disciple said.

"Some say Elijah or Jeremiah," chimed in another.

"Or maybe another prophet," a third added. The disciples didn't mean Jesus was actually one of these people. They meant people thought He was as great as John the Baptist, Elijah and Jeremiah. These men were great heroes to the Jewish people. They followed God with their whole hearts and were even willing to die for Him. As far as the Jewish people were concerned, the highest compliment you could give a man was to say he was one of God's prophets. The disciples thought Jesus would be pleased to know people thought He was a prophet.

Peter waited for Jesus' response. What He said surprised him. **Read Matthew 16:15 to read what Jesus asked next.**

The question stunned the disciples for a moment. Peter thought for a moment.

> **Storytelling Tip:**
> Follow the SonRock Story Starter introduction activity suggested for each story. This discussion activity will help students know what to focus on as the stories are told. Then use the suggested questions and Scripture look-ups included in the story. These questions guide student discovery of Bible story facts. Students will remember what they discover for themselves longer than the things they merely hear a leader tell them

> **Creative Storytelling Option:**
> Photocopy and cut out "Response Cards" (see p. 44). Give one or more cards to volunteers. At time indicated in story, ask students to read cards aloud.

Was Jesus one of the prophets? Peter thought about some of the things he'd seen Jesus do and the things Jesus had said. (Optional: Ask students holding cards 5-8 to read answers aloud.) Peter remembered how Jesus fed 5,000 people with two fish and five small loaves of bread. He remembered walking on the water with Jesus. He remembered the sick people Jesus had healed, the blind people Jesus made to see, the people who couldn't walk when they came to see Jesus who were able to run and jump for joy after Jesus healed them.

That's more than anything I've heard about any prophet doing, Peter may have thought. And Peter remembered all the things Jesus had taught him about God and God's love. Peter remembered the times Jesus went off to be alone and talk with God. *Jesus loves God more than anyone I've ever seen.* Peter thought. *And Jesus has wisdom about God and His love that goes way beyond anything I've heard from any other teacher . . .* Suddenly God helped Peter realize the truth.

The One True Savior

"You are the Savior God promised to send," Peter said.

The Bible does not tell us whether or not the other disciples were surprised that Peter would say this. Even if they thought Jesus was the Savior, it was another thing to say it out loud! Being a prophet was important enough, but there would be only one Savior; and the Jewish people had prayed and waited for the Savior for hundreds of years. He was called the "Savior" because he would save God's people from suffering and trouble. The other disciples wondered what Jesus would say to Peter.

Jesus looked at Peter. "Well, done, Peter," Jesus said. "It was God who revealed this truth to you." **Remember when Jesus gave Peter his new name?**

What does the name "Peter" mean? (Rock.) Jesus said, "I have called you 'Peter' because it is on this rock I will build my church. And NOTHING will destroy that church!" Jesus meant that the people who followed Jesus would have a strong, solid foundation that they could depend on no matter what.

But some people didn't agree with Peter that Jesus was the Savior. They didn't like the things Jesus said and did. So they came up with a plot to get rid of Jesus. Even though He had done nothing wrong, these people managed to get Jesus arrested. They even managed to get Him killed on a cross!

But Jesus didn't stay dead. After Jesus died, He was buried in a tomb. Three days later, when Peter and some of Jesus' other friends went to the tomb, it was empty! Then Jesus came and talked with Peter and the other disciples. Jesus was alive again! Peter was so excited and happy to see his friend and Savior! All the disciples now knew, like Peter did, that Jesus was the Savior. Jesus dying and then living again PROVED it!

After a while, Jesus returned to heaven where He lives today. Peter and the other disciples and all of Jesus' followers since then have obeyed Jesus' command to tell people all over the world that Jesus is the Savior!

Conclusion

Discovering that Jesus is the Savior and that He died and lives today isn't something that was just important for people like Peter. It isn't something that is just important for grownups to know about. It's important for kids, too.

Because Jesus loves you and accepts you, He died and came alive again to be your Savior and to save you from the consequences of breaking God's rules. Knowing this good news about Jesus means that you can depend on Him just like you depend on a strong rock to hold you up. In Romans 10:9 our Bible says, "If you confess with your mouth, 'Jesus is Lord,' and believe in your heart that God raised him from the dead, you will be saved."

When we are saved by Jesus, we become members of God's family forever! (Invite students interested in knowing more about becoming members of God's family to talk with you or another teacher after class. See "Leading a Child to Christ," p. 10.)

3. Apply the Story (10-15 minutes)

Bible Story Review

Students stand together. A volunteer stands with his or her back to the group. Students in group mix themselves up. Volunteer tosses beanbag over shoulder. Student who catches the beanbag answers one of the questions below (also on page 15 of the *Camp Journals*) or chooses a volunteer to answer. That student then becomes the beanbag tosser. Continue until all the questions have been answered.

▶ **According to our story, who had the Jewish people been waiting hundreds of years for?** (The Savior God promised to send.)

▶ **Who did Peter say he believed Jesus was?** (God's promised Savior.) **What do you think are some of the reasons Peter believed this?** (He had seen Jesus do wonderful and amazing things. Peter had seen how much Jesus knows and loves God. God revealed the truth to him.)

▶ **How did Jesus prove He was the Savior?** (He died and rose again.)

Even today, people have different ideas about who Jesus is. Some people think He's not really important because He lived so long ago. Other people think He's a good teacher but not really the Savior. But the Bible tells us the truth about Jesus: He is the Savior who gives us salvation and eternal life. Give students their *Camp Journals*. Have students find "Saved by Jesus" on page 15. **Today the truth we are learning is that the salvation we can receive from Jesus means that we are members of God's family. As members of God's family, we receive eternal life and will live with Jesus now and forever!** As time allows, students respond to question on page 15 of their journals.

Materials

△ *SonRock Tunes CD* and player
△ *Camp Journals*
△ beanbag
△ markers

Memory Verse/Application

Students turn to pages 16-17 of their *Camp Journals* and read verse aloud. **What does this verse tell us about believing who Jesus is and what He has done?** (When we believe Jesus is the Savior, and ask Him to save us, He will.) **What does this verse invite us to do?** (Say that Jesus is Lord and believe that He will save us.) **When this verse talks about being saved, it means that we all need to be saved from the consequences of breaking God's rules. There's a word for breaking God's rules—"sinning." The Bible says the consequence of sinning is death, separation from God. But because Jesus died in our place, and rose again, He proved He was the Savior! Because Jesus is our Savior, we can have salvation and eternal life, living now and forever as members of God's family!**

Students complete "Letter from Jesus" activity. As an alternative to having each student fill in every vowel on his or her paper, ask students to form groups of five. Assign a different vowel to each student. Students fill in all of the blanks with the vowel they are assigned, and then pass paper to the next student. Students continue passing papers until all of the vowels have been filled in and then read the letter from Jesus. Ask questions such as:

▶ **"Salvation" means being made safe or having been rescued from the consequences of our sin. We often use it to describe what happens when we become a member of God's family. What does that mean to you?**

> ### Asking Questions:
> *Third and fourth graders can often give correct answers while not actually understanding what they mean. It's important for children this age to feel competent, and giving the right answer does that. However, there is great value in finding out what students actually understand. Make questions open-ended, not allowing for one-word answers. Such questions help students explain and clarify what they really think.*

▶ Becoming a member of God's family means we will live with Jesus forever. We call that "eternal life." How does it make you feel to know that you can live with Jesus forever?

Because He loves us so much, Jesus made a way for us to have salvation and eternal life. All we have to do is accept His salvation. I'm so glad that each of us can choose to be saved by Jesus!

Prayer

Play "You Will Be Saved" from CD as students take a few minutes to respond to the prayer prompt on page 18 of their journals.

Invite volunteers to share the prayer they've written. Close in prayer, thanking Jesus that He is the Savior who gives us salvation and eternal life when we ask.

Journal Reflections

Here's what worked today:

Here's what needs work for tomorrow:

My Prayer Requests

Notes for Tomorrow:

I was able to share with children what it means to be saved by Jesus when _____

I can follow up with children who showed an interest in becoming members of God's family by _____

A Rooster Crows
Peter Denies Jesus

Scripture

Matthew 26:31-35,69-75; Luke 22:54-62; John 21:1-17

Bible Memory Verse

You are forgiving and good, O Lord, abounding in love to all who call to you. Psalm 86:5

Who Am I?

Even when I sin, Jesus forgives me and gives me a fresh start.

Bible Aims for Each Student

During this session, I may

1. DISCOVER that even though Peter denied Jesus, he was forgiven by Jesus;

2. LIST and DISCUSS steps to forgiveness;

3. ASK Jesus for forgiveness and a fresh start;

4. CHOOSE to receive God's forgiveness and to become a member of God's family, as the Holy Spirit leads.

Teacher's Devotional

It may be easy to judge Peter's actions in today's story by asking, "What was he thinking? Didn't Jesus just warn him that he would deny Him? I would NEVER do that!" Or would you? Peter watched Jesus get arrested, even though He had done nothing wrong. Peter must have been worried about being arrested himself! So yes, Peter denied knowing Jesus. He lied. He was a sinner.

What about you? Aren't you a sinner, too? We all desperately need to be forgiven by Jesus. But not only was Peter forgiven, he was also given a fresh start and commissioned to share Christ's love with others by "feeding His sheep." Jesus is faithful to forgive us (see 1 John 1:9). He won't hold our sins against us (see Psalm 103:9-12).

Consider how precious the gift of forgiveness is for you and receive the fresh start that Christ's forgiveness offers. Pray that your campers will realize their wrong choices, ask Jesus to forgive them and then ask for strength not to repeat the same wrong choices again. Ask Jesus to help you model His forgiveness to the campers in your care.

4 Forgiven by Jesus

1. Set the Story (5-10 minutes)

If you only have 25 minutes for this center, omit Set the Story.

Choose Either **Active Option** or **Table Option**

For either Option, use the conversation ideas in "Talk About" to tie the student activity to the Daily Truth that we are Forgiven by Jesus.

Active Option: Circle Talk

Procedure: Students form two groups with equal numbers. One group forms a circle in the middle of the playing area. The second group forms a circle around the first group. Play music from CD as students walk around their circles, each circle going in the opposite direction. After a few moments, stop music. Students stop walking and face the closest student from the other group. Students tell each other a reason a kid might need forgiveness.

Materials

⚠ *SonRock Tunes CD* and player

For either option, Talk About:

We ask for forgiveness when we're sorry for something we've done.

▶ **When are some times people say they are sorry?** (When they've said something mean. When they've done unkind things.)

▶ **What can make it hard or easy to say "I'm sorry" and ask for forgiveness?**

We all do wrong things. Knowing we've done wrong things can make us feel guilty and sad. But when we are given forgiveness, we don't have to feel bad anymore! Being forgiven means we get a fresh start. Today we're going to talk about how Jesus can give us forgiveness and a fresh start.

Table Option: Time for Forgiveness

Preparation: Photocopy "Time for Forgiveness," making a copy for each student.

Procedure: Students find hidden words in the pictures to complete the acrostic. Ask students to tell the words they found. **These are all words that remind us of what we might think about or feel when we do something wrong.**

Materials

⚠ Time for Forgiveness (p. 45)

⚠ markers

2. Tell the Story (10 minutes)

Materials

⋀ Bibles

⋀ Session 4 Bible Story Posters 1 and 2 from *Poster Pack*

⋀ Post-it Notes

Preparation: Display Session 4 Bible Story Posters. Use Post-it Notes to mark Matthew 26 in students' Bibles. If Bibles are not available for all students, mark your Bible and ask volunteers to read verses as indicated in the story.

A Rooster Crows: Peter Denies Jesus

Matthew 26:31-35,69-75; Luke 22:54-62; John 21:1-17

Today we're going to play an improvisation game. Make a face and pose to express excitement. **What emotion do you think I'm showing?** Volunteers respond. **Now I'm going to call out some emotions. Show me your best expression! You can use your face and your body to show the emotion.** Call out some or all of these emotions: anger, boredom, frustration, excitement, sadness, jealousy, guilt. Pause after each emotion to give kids time to show the emotion. End with the word "guilt." **Great job! You all really know how to show your emotions. The last emotion we showed was guilt. Today we're going to hear about someone who ended up feeling very guilty on the night Jesus was arrested.**

On the Mount of Olives

Peter and the other disciples went with Jesus to a place called the Mount of Olives. They had just celebrated the Passover meal with Jesus and Jesus had said something that upset Peter tremendously. During the meal, Jesus had said one of the disciples would betray Him. *I can't believe any of us would betray Jesus,* Peter must have thought. *We've all seen the amazing things He's done. He's the Savior! Who would betray the Savior?*

But then Jesus said something else that upset Peter, "Friends, before tonight is over, you will all desert Me. You'll even deny that you know Me."

Peter couldn't believe his ears! "Lord, I will NEVER say I don't know You! Even if everyone else leaves You, I never will," Peter said firmly.

Jesus looked at His friend, "Peter, I'm telling you the truth. Before the rooster crows in the morning, you will say that you don't know Me three times."

Peter couldn't believe what Jesus was saying. Peter loved his friend and believed he would do anything for Him. **Read what Peter said in Matthew 26:35.** Peter said he'd DIE before he'd deny knowing Jesus. The other disciples spoke up and said they too would stand by Jesus.

But shortly after that, Jesus was arrested. And all the disciples ran away, just like Jesus had said they would. The disciples were afraid. If Jesus could be arrested when He hadn't done anything wrong, maybe they could be arrested just for KNOWING Him!

In the Courtyard

Even though Peter was scared, he followed the soldiers who took Jesus—but at what he thought was a safe distance. Peter watched as Jesus was taken to the high priest's house to be questioned. Peter couldn't go inside, so he waited outside.

Peter noticed some people gathered around a fire in the courtyard. *It's awfully cold. I'll go by the fire to wait,* he thought to himself. As he warmed himself by a fire, a servant girl looked at Peter. She studied his face for a moment and then seemed to recognize him. She asked, "Hey, aren't you one of the disciples that follows that man being questioned in there?"

Storytelling Tip:

As you tell the story, keep the session's Daily Truth and Who Am I? statements in mind. That way you will be able to emphasize how the story events reinforce the main idea of the session. And through your emphasis, students will more clearly understand and be able to recall each session's Daily Truth and Who Am I? statements.

Creative Storytelling Option:

Ask a volunteer to dress in Bible-times costume and tell the story from a first-person point of view, as if he or she were Peter.

Everyone turned to look at Peter. And Peter froze. He was terrified! **Read Matthew 26:70 to find out what Peter said.** Peter lied. "I have no idea what you're talking about," Peter said sharply.

Now another person spoke up. "Yeah… Sure! I've seen you with Him!"

Peter was desperate. "It wasn't me! I don't know what you people are talking about."

A little while later someone else recognized Peter as one of Jesus' friends. "This guy was with that man. Look at him! You can tell he's from Galilee, same as that Jesus fellow."

This time Peter was really mad. He cursed and yelled, "I am NOT one of Jesus' friends," Peter yelled. "I don't know the man you're talking about!"

Just then, a rooster crowed. Suddenly, Peter remembered Jesus' words, "Before the rooster crows in the morning, you will say that you don't know Me three times." The guilt of his denial crashed down on Peter like a heavy hammer. Peter stumbled away from the fire. He went outside the gates and cried bitter tears. *I can't believe what I've done! I couldn't even admit that I knew Him, let alone that He is my friend and Savior.* Peter felt miserable. He must have wondered if Jesus would ever forgive him.

The Bible tells us that after His arrest, Jesus was killed and buried in a tomb. Peter was miserable. But on the third day after all this happened, some women told Peter that the tomb was empty! Peter ran to see the empty tomb. Jesus was alive! Peter actually saw Jesus several times after He rose from the tomb.

On the Water

One of those times was when Peter and several of the disciples had been out fishing all night long. But they hadn't caught a single fish. As they neared shore, Peter saw a man standing on the beach. The man called out to them, "Friends, haven't you any fish?"

"No," the disciples answered.

Then the man said something strange. "Throw your net over the right side of the boat. You'll find fish there." Peter looked at the other disciples and shrugged. *It can't hurt to try!* He may have thought. So they tossed the net, SPLASH, into the water on the right side of the boat.

When they tried to pull the net in again, it was so heavy with fish, they couldn't budge it! *Hey! This seems pretty familiar,* Peter thought, remembering the time when Jesus called Peter to follow Him. Peter looked over again at the man on the beach. So did another disciple, John. Suddenly John yelled, "It is the LORD!"

Jesus! It's Jesus on the shore! Peter was so happy and excited, he jumped right into the water and swam to shore to see Jesus. The rest of the disciples followed in the boat. When they got to the shore, they saw that Jesus had made a fire and started cooking breakfast. "Bring in those fish you just caught," Jesus said. Peter climbed back on board the boat and helped the other disciples drag the net ashore. Even though it was loaded down with fish, the net didn't tear. "Come and eat!" Jesus said. Peter was thrilled to see Jesus, but he also probably still felt guilty about having denied Jesus.

Jesus knew exactly how Peter was feeling. And He wanted Peter to know that he was forgiven. After they had eaten, Jesus and Peter talked together. **What do you think Peter was hoping Jesus would say?**

"Peter, do you love Me?" Jesus asked.

Peter was glad to be able to tell Jesus, "Yes, Lord, You know that I love You."

"Feed My sheep," Jesus said. And He said it three times! Jesus meant that Peter was to help His followers know more about God's love. Jesus didn't give up on Peter when Peter sinned.

Conclusion

Jesus loved Peter and gave him an important job to do. Best of all, Peter knew that Jesus had forgiven him and that he could make a fresh start with Jesus! Jesus doesn't give up on us either. His forgiveness is as reliable as a big strong rock. We can know for certain that Jesus loves us, even when we do wrong things.

In Psalm 86:5 our Bible says, "You are forgiving and good, O Lord, abounding in love to all who call to you." All we have to do is ask, and Jesus will forgive us.

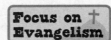

When we ask for His forgiveness, Jesus forgives us AND gives us a fresh start as members of God's family. (Invite students interested in knowing more about becoming members of God's family to talk with you or another teacher after class. See "Leading a Child to Christ," p. 10.)

4 Forgiven by Jesus

3. Apply the Story (10-15 minutes)

Bible Story Review

Divide class into groups of no more than four. Give each group a coin. Volunteer in each group flips coin at your signal. Students in groups whose coin lands heads up answer one of the questions below (also on page 19 of the *Camp Journals*). Repeat until all the questions have been answered.

Materials

⚠ *SonRock Tunes CD* and player

⚠ *Camp Journals*

⚠ coins

⚠ markers

▶ **Why did Peter need to be forgiven?** (Broke his promise to Jesus and said three times he didn't know Jesus.)

▶ **How did Jesus show Peter he was forgiven?** (Helped him catch fish. Asked him to feed His sheep. Didn't give up on Peter.)

▶ **What do you think was the most important part of this story? Why?**

▶ **What might make it hard to make a fresh start?** (Feeling like your friends will make fun of you if you change. Feeling like you've done something so bad, the situation can't be changed.)

Even though Peter had denied Him, Jesus forgave Peter and gave him a fresh start. A fresh start doesn't mean starting our lives over again in a new place with new names and new friends. It means that Jesus will help us start over again with new actions and attitudes. Have students find "Forgiven by Jesus" on page 19. **Today we're learning the truth that when we ask for Jesus' forgiveness, He will forgive us. Jesus helps us love and obey Him.** As time allows, students respond to question on page 19 of their journals.

Memory Verse/Application

Students turn to pages 20-21 in their *Camp Journals* and read verse aloud. **When our verses say to "call to God," it means to pray and ask for God's help. Because Jesus loves us so much, we can call on Him for help and forgiveness. Along with His forgiveness, Jesus gives us a fresh start! That means Jesus doesn't remember the wrong things we've done. He doesn't hold those things against us. What a great gift!**

As students complete "Trail of Forgiveness" activity, ask questions such as:

▶ **According to our *Camp Journal* pages, what are the four steps to forgiveness?** (Admit our sins. Accept forgiveness. Ask for help not to sin again. Thank Jesus for His forgiveness.)

▶ **How do we know Jesus will forgive us?** (Our memory verse tells us. Because Jesus loves us and keeps His promises.)

▶ **Why is it important to ask for help not to sin again?** (If we're really sorry for the wrong things we've done, we don't want to do them again.)

▶ **What are some ways to thank Jesus for His forgiveness?** (Not do the same wrong things over and over. Pray and say "Thank You.")

Jesus will always forgive us when we ask. And by following the steps of forgiveness, we can get help not to sin again and also thank Jesus for His forgiveness!

Discussion Tip:
The most effective teachers do as much careful listening and observing as they do talking. Effective teachers also limit much of their talking to asking questions designed to help them better understand their students.

Prayer

Play "You Are Forgiving" from CD as students take a few minutes to respond to the prayer prompt on page 22 of their journals.

We can thank Jesus for His forgiveness and also that His forgiveness gives us a fresh start. If you would like forgiveness for something you've done, you can ask Jesus now by praying silently. Close in prayer, thanking Jesus for forgiving everyone who asked and for giving them a fresh start.

Journal Reflections

Here's what worked today:

Here's what needs work for tomorrow:

My Prayer Requests

Notes for Tomorrow

I saw examples of forgiveness today when

I can demonstrate Jesus' love and forgiveness when

Lame Man Leaping
Peter Helps a Lame Man

Scripture
Acts 3

Bible Memory Verse
For we are God's workmanship, created in Christ Jesus to do good works, which God prepared in advance for us to do. Ephesians 2:10

Who Am I?
I can live for Jesus and do the good things He has planned for me to do.

Bible Aims for Each Student
During this session, I may

1. TELL that Peter demonstrated Jesus' love and power when he helped the lame man;

2. DISCOVER what Jesus gives to help us live for Him as His children;

3. ASK Jesus to give me strength to live for Him and do the good things He has planned;

4. CHOOSE to receive God's forgiveness and to become a member of God's family, as the Holy Spirit leads.

Teacher's Devotional
It is hard to see this exciting week come to a close. But for your campers who have chosen to live for Jesus, the excitement is just beginning. Observe their wonder as they discover Jesus' power displayed through Peter, a regular guy, when a lame man is healed! Jesus is the same yesterday, today and tomorrow (see Hebrews 13:8). Just as He allowed Peter to display His power, who knows how He wants to display His power through you and the campers at SonRock Kids Camp!

Think of the ways you have seen the power of Jesus at work this week. When you have shown love to the difficult-to-love child, you have seen God's power at work. When a child or adult has made a decision to live for Jesus, you have seen the power of Jesus at work. When a child has reached out to someone in need, you have seen the power of Jesus at work.

As you end the week with your campers, point out the ways you have seen the power of Jesus displayed around SonRock Kids Camp and remind them that God created them with a purpose to do good things (see Ephesians 2:10).

1. Set the Story (5-10 minutes)

If you only have 25 minutes for this center, omit Set the Story.

Choose Either Active Option or Table Option
For either Option, use the conversation ideas in "Talk About" to tie the student activity to the Daily Truth that we are Living for Jesus.

Active Option: Paper Toss

Preparation: Open sleeping bag and place it on the floor in an open area of the room.

Procedure: Students stand several feet away from sleeping bag, crumple a piece of paper and then toss paper over their shoulders at the sleeping bag. For every paper that lands on the sleeping bag, students name an attitude or action someone can do that makes camp a great place to be (being happy or friendly, helping pick up trash, giving someone else first turn to play a game, sharing a snack, showing kindness, etc.). For each paper that lands off the sleeping bag, students name an attitude or action someone can do that makes camp less fun (saying mean things, taking cuts in line, cheating at a game, etc.) and then tells something that person could do instead that would be a better thing to do.

Materials
△ sleeping bag
△ scrap paper

For either option, Talk About:

Every day we learn about people when we see what they do and hear what they say. And people learn about us by our attitudes and actions, too!

▶ **What are some words to describe different attitudes people might have?** (Kind. Caring. Mean. Considerate. Selfish. Bossy. Thoughtful.)

▶ **What is an action someone who is (selfish) might do?** Repeat for some of the other responses given.

▶ **If someone is (caring) to you, what does that tell you about the kind of person they are?** Repeat for some of the other responses given.

Today we'll talk about how our actions and attitudes can say a lot about who we are and what we think is important. Our actions not only can help people learn about who we are, but also whether or not we are "Living for Jesus."

Table Option: Straight Arrows

Preparation: Photocopy "Straight Arrows," making a copy for each student.

Procedure: Students color the arrows that show attitudes or actions that would make SonRock Kids Camp a great place.

Materials
△ Straight Arrows (p. 46)
△ markers

2. Tell the Story (10 minutes)

Preparation: Display Session 5 Bible Story Posters. Use Post-it Notes to mark Acts 3 in students' Bibles. If Bibles are not available for all students, mark your Bible and ask volunteers to read verses as indicated in the story.

Materials

◮ Bibles

◮ Session 5 Bible Story Posters 1 and 2 from *Poster Pack*

◮ Post-it Notes

Lame Man Leaping: Peter Helps a Lame Man Acts 3

What are abilities or talents? Volunteers respond. **Abilities and talents are special characteristics given to us by God. Everyone has them! Some of us are good at sports; some of us write well; some of us play musical instruments or sing. Today we'll act out different abilities or talents—without speaking! Guess what each one is.** Ask a volunteer to whisper an ability or talent to you. Pantomime what it is until students guess correctly. As time allows, different volunteers act out abilities and talents. **Well, today we're going to hear about a very special thing God gave Peter the ability to do.**

A Beggar

After Jesus died, rose again and returned to heaven, Peter and the other disciples told more and more people about Him. And those people told people! People from many countries heard about Jesus and became members of God's family. Peter was happy and excited to tell others about his amazing friend Jesus!

One afternoon, Peter and John, another of Jesus' disciples, were in Jerusalem. They decided to go to the Temple to pray. There were often beggars outside the Temple, since the beggars knew people would give them money to try to please God.

One beggar came every day to the Temple. **Read Acts 3:2 to hear more about this man.** The man's legs didn't work, and they hadn't worked for his entire life! He was never able to walk or run or play as a child. Now as an adult, he couldn't get a job and earn money. All he could do was beg for money. He couldn't even get there on his own; others had to help him.

Peter saw the man being carried to the Temple gate, where he was put down to beg for money. The man asked Peter and John for money, just like he asked everyone. Most people either ignored the man or gave him money without really looking at him. But Peter and John looked straight at the man. And Peter felt compassion for him. Peter wanted to help him!

A Helping Hand

Peter said, "Look at me." The man looked and then held up his beggar's bowl, expecting Peter to give him some money.

Peter shook his head. "No, I don't have any money to give you," he said. "But what I do have, I give to you! In the name of Jesus, get up and walk!" Then Peter reached out his big strong hand and grabbed the man's right hand, pulling him to his feet! To the man's great surprise, he didn't fall down! Instead, he felt the strange sensation of strength in ankles that had never held him up before.

What?! The man must have wondered. **How do you think the man must have felt to stand up for the first time in his life?** The man didn't just stand up, he started to walk!

Storytelling Tip:
Know your story well enough to talk with your students rather than read to them. When your eyes are not tied to the words of the story, you are free to focus on the faces of the students in your class. This will both engage the students' attention and minimize disruptions.

Creative Storytelling Option:
Before telling the story, tape a large sheet of paper to wall (or use a white board or large pad on easel). Give each student a sheet of paper and a pencil. Ask students to fold their paper into half three times to create eight sections on the page. As you tell the story, draw or have a helper draw each sketch, referring to Bible Story Pictures on page 47. Students copy sketches. (Hint: If you are using paper, use a pencil to lightly draw the pictures in advance. Trace over the pictures with a marker.)

"Praise God!" the man shouted. He took a small step. And then another. And another! He took a small, careful jump. And then a bigger jump! And then he started jumping up and down with excitement. "I'm healed! I can walk! Praise God!" the man shouted.

Peter and John were happy to have helped the man. They continued walking into the Temple and the man went right along with them. The people in the Temple turned to stare.

"What's all the noise about?" a man asked, straining to get a better look.

"Hey! Isn't that the man who sits by the gate, begging for money?" one man asked, pointing. "He's never walked a day in his life!"

"I know!" Another man said, staring in amazement. "I helped carry him here!"

"You don't have to carry me anymore!" The healed man shouted. "I'm healed! Praise the Lord!"

The healed man continued walking with Peter and John, running and jumping and shouting for joy. The people began to form a crowd around the healed man, Peter and John. The people had all seen that man every day at the Temple. They KNEW he couldn't walk, yet here he was, and he was healed.

A Crowd of Believers

"It's those two fellows who healed the lame man," the people started to whisper. "They must be miracle healers!"

Peter began to feel uncomfortable. *They think I healed the man!* Peter thought. *I don't have the power to heal ANYBODY! I'd better tell them the truth,* he decided. *I don't want people to think I have any sort of magical powers!*

Peter turned to the people. "Why are you so surprised?" he asked. "Do you really think that WE," pointing to himself and John, "have the power to heal people? We didn't heal this man." Peter was thrilled to have a chance to tell so many people about Jesus. "Do you remember Jesus?" he asked.

Not too long before this Jesus had been killed. The people remembered Him. Some had believed Jesus was a criminal and some believed Him to be the Savior. ALL of the people had heard stories about God's promised Savior. They had prayed and waited like their parents and ancestors before them. They knew that the Savior would suffer so that they could be forgiven for the wrong things they did.

"Well, I am here to tell you that even though Jesus was killed, God has raised Jesus from the dead. And it is by HIS power that this man was healed!" continued Peter.

Many people were shocked to hear that Jesus, whom they thought was a criminal, was responsible for this great miracle. Peter knew they felt this way. "Don't feel bad about what you've done," Peter went on to say. "You didn't really understand who Jesus was. Jesus IS the Savior! He is the One the prophets said would come and suffer. He suffered and died on the cross. But He didn't stay dead! We know," Peter said, indicating himself and John. "We are witnesses! We've seen Him alive! It was Jesus and His power that healed this man and made him able to walk!" **Read what else Peter said in Acts 3:16.**

Peter then told the people to repent—to turn away from sin and start obeying God. The Bible tells us that on that day thousands of people came to accept God's love and become members of God's family. Peter's heart filled with joy to see so many people excited to hear about Jesus and His love.

Conclusion

The crowd of people became a crowd of believers because of what Peter did and said. Peter's words and actions showed that he was a follower of Jesus. Peter wanted to do good things to love and obey Jesus. In Ephesians 2:10, our Bibles say, "For we are God's workmanship, created in Christ Jesus to do good works, which God prepared in advance for us to do." God has planned good things for each of us to do. You might think that no one pays attention to what kids do or say. But every day, what you say and what you do shows whether or not you are following Jesus.

When we become members of God's family, we know that we can build our lives on the solid rock of Jesus' love. As followers of Jesus, we know without any doubts that we have been accepted by Jesus, we are protected by Jesus, we have been saved by Jesus and we are forgiven by Jesus. It is then time to LIVE FOR JESUS. When we live for Jesus, others will see His love in us and they may choose to become members of God's family, too!

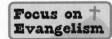 It's important for each person to decide about becoming a member of God's family. No one else can make this decision for you. (Invite students interested in knowing more about becoming members of God's family to talk with you or another teacher after class. See "Leading a Child to Christ," p. 10.)

3. Apply the Story (10-15 minutes)

Bible Story Review

Behind your back, hold up from zero to five fingers. At your signal, students guess the number you chose by holding up their fingers. Students whose number matches yours answers one of the questions below (also on page 23 of the *Camp Journals*). Repeat until all of the questions have been answered.

▷ **What did the people in the Temple learn from Peter's words and actions?** (Jesus is alive and the One who healed the man who couldn't walk. Jesus is the Savior. They can become members of God's family.)

▷ **How do good words and right actions help people learn about Jesus?** (When people ask us about the things we do, we can tell them we are living for Jesus.)

▷ **What are things kids your age do that show they love and obey Jesus?**

Peter did his best to live for Jesus by showing his love for Jesus in the actions he did and the words he said. Have students find "Living for Jesus" on page 23. **Today we're learning the truth that when we live for Jesus, our words and actions will show how much we love Him!** As time allows, students respond to question on page 23 of their journals.

Materials

⚠ *SonRock Tunes CD* and player
⚠ *Camp Journals*
⚠ markers

Memory Verse/Application

Students turn to pages 24-25 of their *Camp Journals* and read verse aloud. **What do you think is the main idea of this verse? Jesus has a plan for each of us. We were created to do good things for Jesus and for others. Every day, Jesus will give us the strength we need to do the good things He has planned for us.**

As students complete "Things I Learned at Camp" activity, ask questions such as:

▷ **What are some of the good works Jesus wants us to do?** (Don't tease my younger brother or sister. Read the Bible. Don't swear or lie. Be honest when parents ask if you've done something or not.)

▷ **What are ways we can know what good works Jesus has planned for us?** (Follow the example of people in the Bible. Pay attention to the instructions in Bible verses. Pray to Jesus. Ask parents or teachers.)

▷ **When are some times you might need Jesus' help to do good works and live for Him?** (When friends want me to do something wrong. When I'm angry or tired. When someone is being mean.)

Every day Jesus will give us strength to do the good things He has planned for us to do. All we have to do is ask for His help.

> ### Teaching Tip:
> *A student's words and actions are clues to his or her comprehension. Watch a student's facial expression and body language. Listen carefully. Avoid letting your mind race ahead to what you want to say next. Instead, respond to a student by rephrasing his or her comments to be sure you understood. By carefully listening, you can determine what Bible truths need reinforcing.*

Prayer

Play "The Trail of Life" from CD as students take a few minutes to respond to the prayer prompt on page 26 of their journals.

Invite volunteers to share the prayer they wrote on their *Camp Journal* pages. **Let's pray and ask Jesus to give us strength to live for Him.** Lead students in prayer, thanking Jesus for the good things He has planned for us to do and the strength to do those good things. After all volunteers have prayed, close prayer by praising Jesus for His love and guidance.

Journal Reflections

God has answered my prayers this week by _____

My Prayer

I have seen children and leaders living for Jesus this week when _____

I want to live for Jesus by _____

Cabin Fever Maze

It's the first day of camp and Madison must find her way to cabin #2. Use the map to help Madison find her way. Along the path, you will find words. Write the words in order on the lines at the bottom of the page to read an important message.

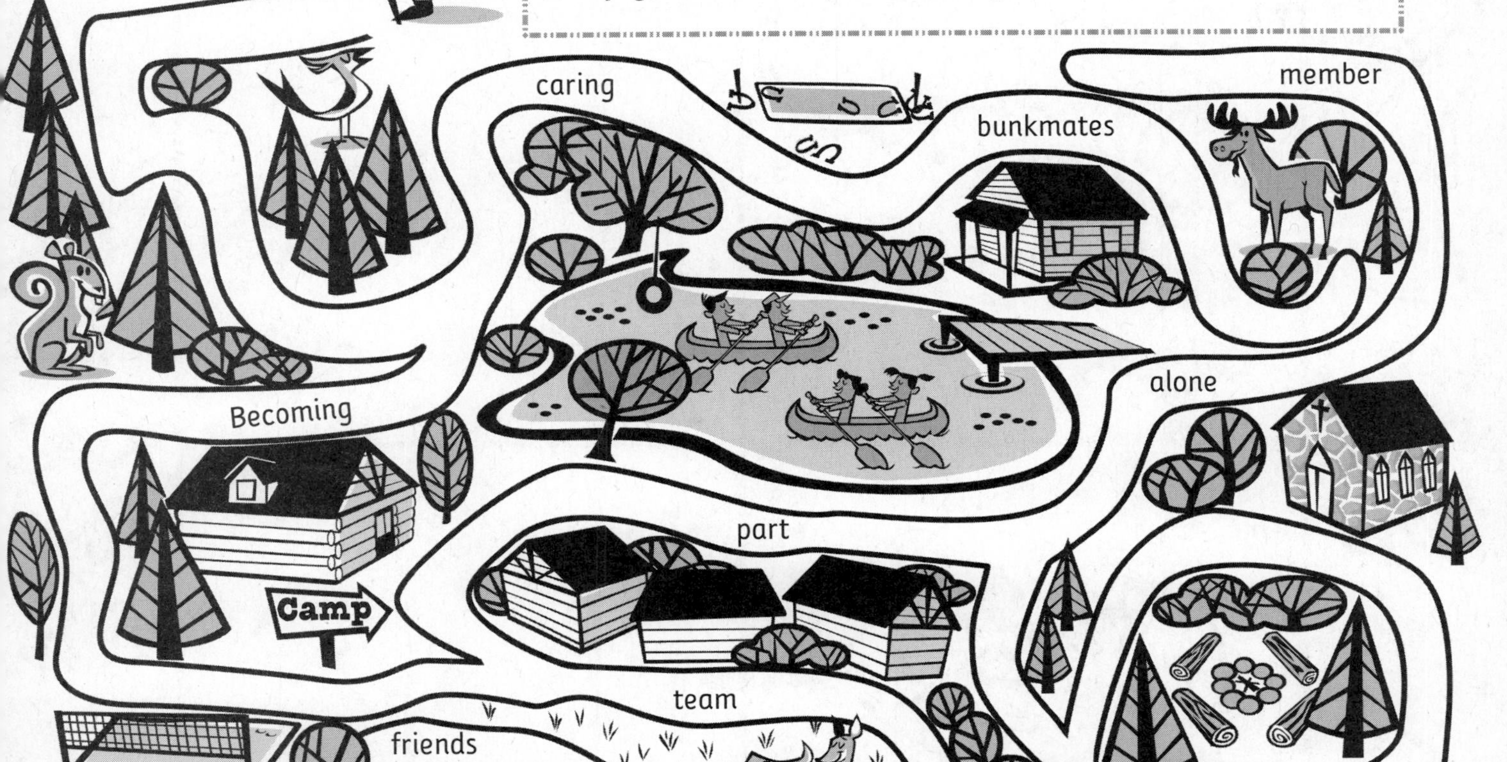

caring

bunkmates

member

Becoming

alone

part

team

friends

group

rejected

approval

counselor

accepted

receive

_____ a _____ of the _____ means I've been _____ .

Complete the Comic

For each of the comics below, draw in the blank square what you would do to protect yourself. Draw your own comic strip in the last set of boxes. If you need ideas, look at the pictures around the edge of the paper.

Swimming Rules

Help the lifeguard by unscrambling the scrambled words in the Swimming Rules sign. Some of the letters have been filled in for you.

Swimming Rules

1. No mgiwsimn s _ i _ _ i _ _ unless

draugefil l _ _ e _ _ _ _ d is

eenprst p _ _ _ _ n _.

2. No nirngun r u _ _ _ _ n _ or

hurog r _ _ _ _ _ sngiuoh h o _ _ i _.

3. No dvniig d _ v _ _ _.

4. veaeL L _ _ _ _ v _ area at the first sign of

nlghtngii l i _ h _ _ i _ _.

5. No asgls g _ a _ _ or ugm g _ _ _ _ allowed.

6. Keep the aetg g _ _ _ _ _ cdsloe c l _ _ _ _.

7. eavH H _ _ _ _ nfu f _ _ _!

Which is the most important rule? Why?

Response Cards

1 John the Baptist

5 Feeding 5,000 People

2 Elijah

6 Walking on Water

3 Jeremiah

7 Healing the Sick

4 Another Prophet

8 Wisdom About God

Time for Forgiveness

Find the hidden words in each picture.
Use the words to fill in the blank lines

Name: _____

Straight Arrows

Read the attitudes and actions below. Circle the arrows that have actions or attitudes that would make SonRock Kids Camp a great place to be. Draw an X through the other arrows. Write your own ideas of good actions or attitudes on the blank lines.

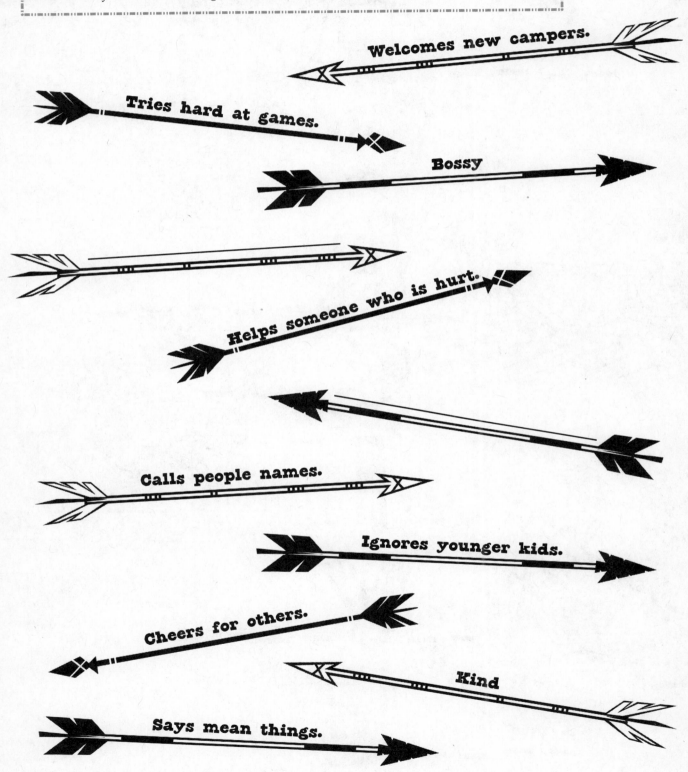

Welcomes new campers.

Tries hard at games.

Bossy

Helps someone who is hurt.

Calls people names.

Ignores younger kids.

Cheers for others.

Kind

Says mean things.

Bible Story Pictures

Follow the directions below to draw sketches at appropriate times in story.

1. Draw "X" for legs; add stick figure.

2. Draw bowl from "O" and "U."

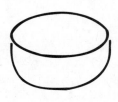

3. Make faces from "P" and "J."

4. Draw leaping figure from "N."

5. Draw man's face near Peter's and John's.

6. Add "C"s for crowd around Peter, John and man.

7. Print "GOD"; add burst from "V"s.

8. Add smiling faces to crowd.

Let Kids Know that Jesus Is the Rock

This *Bible Story Center Guide* features easy 3-step lessons.

Inside You'll Find...
- Attention-Grabbing Activities
- Creative Storytelling Options
- Meaningful Discussion Questions
- Time-Saving Reproducible Pages

Make VBS fun last all summer long!

Rock-Solid Followers, a 13-lesson adventure, features 13 truths about Jesus. The fun and excitement of an outdoor adventure camp is combined with the discovery of who we are in Jesus Christ, and the richness and the promise of His love for us. Building on this solid foundation, this course also challenges children to be excited about missions at home and around the world.

Use it midweek, second-hour, or anytime you have a group of kids. For ages 3-12.

Rock-Solid Followers
ISBN-13: 978-0-8307-5114-3
ISBN-10: 0-8307-5114-9

ISBN-13: 978-0-8307-4738-2
ISBN-10: 0-8307-4738-9

9 780830 747382

90000

Gospel Light VBS
Fun in the Son!™
www.gospellightvbs.com

Signatures

ALL SMILES

PRACTICE BOOK

HARCOURT
BRACE

THIS BOOK IS THE PROPERTY OF:

STATE_____

PROVINCE_____

COUNTY_____

PARISH_____

SCHOOL DISTRICT_____

OTHER_____

Book No. _____

Enter information
in spaces
to the left as
instructed

ISSUED TO	Year Used	CONDITION	
		ISSUED	RETURNED
....	....		
....	....		
....	....		
....	....		
....	....		
....	....		
....	....		
....	....		

PUPILS to whom this textbook is issued must not write on any page or mark any part of it in any way, consumable textbooks excepted.

1. Teachers should see that the pupil's name is clearly written in ink in the spaces above in every book issued.
2. The following terms should be used in recording the condition of the book: New; Good; Fair; Poor; Bad.